I AM...

WHO GOD SAYS I AM

Biblical affirmations book for little boys

VICTORY LIFE
MEDIA

JERRY & LAETITIA
BONSU

Published in France by VICTORY LIFE MEDIA an imprint of JBM

JERRY BONSU MINISTRIES
http://www.jerrybonsu.org

VLM books may be ordered through booksellers or by visiting **www.jerrybonsu.org**. VLM Speakers Bureau provides a wide range of authors for speaking events. To find out more, email us: **victorylifemedia@gmail.com**.

French National Library-in-Publication Data
Dépôt légal: 10/2018

Book cover art by Victory Life Media Team

Printed in the United States of America

ISBN: 978-2-9565725-0-3

For further information or permission, contact us on the Internet:

VICTORY LIFE MEDIA "Empowering our Generation for the next Generation" **www.victorylifemedia.com**.

To Janelle & Janessa… Each of you is so fearfully and wonderfully made. We look forward to the wonderful works that our Heavenly Father will work through you.

To our friend and brother, Erick Agoro Simba (Founder of Christian Best Camps of Kenya) and his wife Yasmine… May God bless you both always and provide you the courage to continue the great works you and team CBCK are doing for this generation for the next generation!

INTRODUCTION

Hello!

My name is Janelle Kierra Bonsu but all my friends and family call me "Kiki". This is my little sister Janessa Kimani Bonsu, and we call her "Kime". We are very happy that you are going to read this book, "I AM... Who God says I AM" Biblical affirmations, written with our parents.

What is affirmation?! An affirmation is a compliment that you give to yourself. Do you know that the God of the entire universe, the GREAT I AM knows your name? And He calls you friend?! He said in His Book (The Bible) that He has a GREAT plan for your life. A very Big plans!!!... with joy, peace and love! Read the wonderful words He says about you. Repeat them, and get ready to feel good, better, special and unique!

Aa

Awsome

I am awsome. I am amazing.
I am what God says I am.
Chosen by Jesus, named by Jesus.
Saved in Jesus, always with Jesus.
I am blessed, you see
I am, **awsome** me.

*"You formed the way I think and feel.
You put me together in my mother's womb.
I praise you because you made me in such a wonderful way.
I know how amazing that was! "*

Psalm 139:13-14 (ERV)

Bb

Blessed

I am blessed.
I am blessed coming in, and blessed going out.
I am the head and not the tail.
I am above and not beneath.
I am blessed, you see
*I am, **blessed** me.*

"Taste and see that the Lord is good;
blessed is the one who takes refuge in him."

Psalm 34:8

Cc

Courageous

I am courageous. I am Bold.
With God I am fearless.
I can do all things through Christ
who strengthens me.
I am blessed, you see
I am, **courageous** me.

"The LORD is my light and my salvation whom shall I fear?
The LORD is the stronghold of my life
of whom shall I be afraid?"

Psalm 27:1

Dd

Destined

I am destined.
Destined for greatness, destined for success.
God has a perfect plans for my life,
plans to give me hope and a future.
I am blessed, you see
*I am, **destined** me.*

"For I know the plans I have for you," declares the Lord,
"plans to prosper you and not to harm you, plans to give
you hope and a future."

Jeremiah 29:11

Ee

Enough

I am enough.
I am whole and complete.
I am who God says I am,
I have what God says I have
And I can do what God says I can.
I am blessed, you see
*I am, **enough** me*

"I can be content in any and every situation through the
Anointed One who is my power and strength."

Philippians 4:13-14 (VOICE)

Ff

Free

I am free. Free to be me.
I am free from fear,
I am free from doubt.
Where the Spirit of the Lord is,
there is freedom.
I am blessed, you see
*I am, **free** me*

"It is for freedom that Christ has set us free. Stand firm,
then, and do not let yourselves be burdened again
by a yoke of slavery."

Galatians 5:1

Gg

Generous

I am generous.
I am cheerful giver.
I believe it is better to give than to receive.
I love seeing people happy.
I am blessed, you see
*I am, **generous** me*

"A generous person will prosper;
whoever refreshes others will be refreshed."

Proverbs 11:25

Hh

Happy

I am happy. Happy to be me.
I am in charge of how I feel and
today I am choosing happiness.
The joy of the Lord is my strength.
I am blessed, you see
*I am, **happy** me.*

"Take delight in the Lord, and he will give
you the desires of your heart."

Psalm 37:4

Ii

Intelligent

I am intelligent.
God is my source of understanding,
knowledge and wisdom.
I work with excellence.
I give 100%, and nothing less.
I am blessed, you see
*I am, **intelligent** me.*

"The fear of the LORD is the beginning of wisdom; A good understanding have all those who do His commandments; His praise endures forever."

Psalm 111:10

Jj

Joyful

I am joyful.
God is my joy, my comfort, and my all.
In His presence, there is fullness of joy.
He puts gladness in my heart everyday.
I am blessed, you see
*I am, **joyful** me.*

"Rejoice in the Lord always.
I will say it again: Rejoice!"

Philippians 4:4

Kk

Kind

I am kind.
I am friendly to all.
I radiate love and compassion.
I love God and I love people.
I am blessed, you see
I am, **kind** *me.*

"Be kind and helpful to one another, tender-hearted [compassionate, understanding], forgiving one another [readily and freely], just as God in Christ also forgave you."

Ephesians 4:32 (AMP)

17

Ll

Love

I am love. I am loved.
Honoured, and treasured by Jesus.
My family, friends and teachers
love me for who I am.
I am blessed, you see
*I am, **love** me.*

"But God demonstrates his own love for us in this:
While we were still sinners, Christ died for us."

Romans 5:8

Mm

Miracle

I am miracle.
I thank God for blessing me
with life every day.
I am a blessing to my generation.
I am blessed, you see
*I am, **miracle** me.*

"Before I formed you in the womb I knew you,
before you were born I set you apart; I appointed
you as a prophet to the nations."

Jeremiah 1:5

Nn

Needed

I am needed.
Needed by my family, my friends,
my school, and my community.
I make a difference everywhere I go.
I am blessed, you see
*I am, **needed** me.*

"You are the light of the world. A town built on a hill cannot be hidden. Neither do people light a lamp and put it under a bowl. Instead they put it on its stand, and it gives light to everyone in the house. In the same way, let your light shine before others, that they may see your good deeds and glorify your Father in heaven."

Matthew 5:14-16

Oo

Obedient

I am obedient.
I obey God. I obey my parents in
all things. God says: "Children, obey your
parents in the Lord: for this is right."
I am blessed, you see
*I am, **obedient** me.*

"Children, obey your parents in the Lord, for this is right."

Ephesians 6:1

Pp

Protected

I am protected.
I am divinely protected by God
God is my refuge and strength, always
ready to help in times of trouble.
I am blessed, you see
I am, **protected** me.

"Be strong and courageous. Do not be afraid or terrified
because of them, for the Lord your God goes with you;
he will never leave you nor forsake you."

Deuteronomy 31:6

Qq

Qualified

I am qualified. Qualified by God.
Though others may reject me,
I am favored and choosen by God.
Yes! I am a part of the royal family of God.
I am blessed, you see
I am, **qualified** me.

"…for you are a chosen people. You are royal priests, a holy
nation, God's very own possession. As a result, you can show
others the goodness of God, for he called you out of the
darkness into his wonderful light."

1 Peter 2:9 (NLT)

Rr

Respectful

I am respectful.
I treat other people the way
I want to be treated. I show caring and
respect for others through good manners.
I am blessed, you see
*I am, **respectful** me.*

"Do not forget to show hospitality to strangers,
for by so doing some people have shown hospitality
to angels without knowing it."

Hebrews 13:2

Ss

Strong

I am strong.
In Christ I am more than a conqueror.
He has changed me into a champion,
enabling me to do exploits in His Name.
I am blessed, you see
I am, **strong** me.

"Yet even in the midst of all these things, we triumph over them
all, for God has made us to be more than conquerors, and his
demonstrated love is our glorious victory over everything!"

Romans 8:37 (TPT)

Tt

Thankful

I am thankful. I am also grateful.
I am grateful that God's plan for my life
has never changed. I am grateful for the
favor of God that is on my life.
I am blessed, you see
*I am, **thankful** me.*

"Give thanks in all circumstances; for this is
God's will for you in Christ Jesus."

1 Thessalonians 5:18

Uu

Unique

I am unique.
I am also special and valuable.
God designed me the way I am for a purpose.
Everything about me is unique and
everything about me matters.
I am blessed, you see
I am, **unique** me.

"For he chose us in him before the creation of the world
to be holy and blameless in his sight. In love"

Ephesians 1:4

Vv

Victorious

I am victorious.
I am an overcomer in Jesus.
I have the mind of a winner, the heart of
a champion, the spirit of a conqueror.
I am blessed, you see
*I am, **victorious** me.*

"For everyone born of God overcomes the world. This is the
victory that has overcome the world, even our faith."

1 John 5:4

Ww

I am wise.
I am wise in Christ Jesus.
I am full of the wisdom of God.
And that wisdom is in my
heart and in my mouth.
I am blessed, you see
I am, **wise** me.

"It is because of him that you are in Christ Jesus, who has
become for us wisdom from God – that is, our
righteousness, holiness and redemption."

1 Corinthians 1:30

Xx

Xtraordinary

I am eXtraordinary.
God made me perfect in every way.
I am eXceptional.
I am blessed, you see
I am, **eXtraordinary** me.

"Then God said, "Let us make human beings in our image and likeness. And let them rule over the fish in the sea and the birds in the sky, over the tame animals, over all the earth, and over all the small crawling animals on the earth."

Genesis 1:26 (NCV)

Yy

Yearning

I am Yearning.
Yearning for God, yearning for
Jesus, yearning for Holy Spirit.
That is why I read my Bible
and pray everyday.
I am blessed, you see
*I am, **yearning** me*

"The Lord is good to those whose hope is in him,
to the one who seeks him;"

Lamentations 3:25

Zz

Zealous

I am zealous.
Zealous for God and His kingdom.
I love God with all my heart, with all
my soul and with all my mind.
I thank God for loving me first
I am blessed, you see
*I am, **zealous** me.*

"Therefore, my dear brothers and sisters, stand firm.
Let nothing move you. Always give yourselves fully
to the work of the Lord, because you know that
your labor in the Lord is not in vain."

1 Corinthians 15:58

Write more affirmations about yourself... then share with your family, friends, and your teacher! ☺

_____

_____

_____

_____

_____

_____

_____

_____

_____

_____

_____

_____

_____

BOOKS & CD'S BY JERRY BONSU

* PUSH

* The Path to Victory

* Dear Dreamer

* God Is Up To Something Great

* Step Into Your Purpose

* Courageous Faith

* The Power Of I AM

* The Power Of I AM (Audio Book)

* I AM Who God Says I AM

* The Lord Is My Shepherd

* Victory Noise (Album)

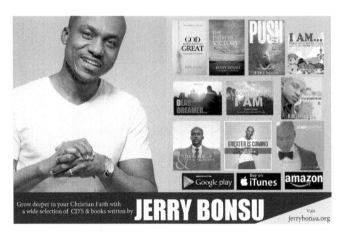

Order these inspiring products and more by visiting
www.jerrybonsu.org and be sure to join us on Facebook, Twitter &
Instagram for more inspirational words.

WWW.JERRYBONSU.ORG

Connect With Jerry!

Website: JerryBonsu.org
Speaking engagements: bookjerry@jerrybonsu.org
Facebook: Facebook.com/jerrybonsuministries
Instagram: Instagram.com/jerrybonsu
Twitter: Twitter.com/jerrybonsu
Youtube: Youtube.com/jerrybonsu
PUSH Conference: Jerrybonsu.org/Push
To join the mailing list: JerryBonsu.org

VICTORY LIFE
MEDIA

Made in the USA
Middletown, DE
26 April 2023

29509340R00022